THEMES
for early years
PHOTOCOPIABLES

D0183091

S   S

EDITOR

Susan Howard

ASSISTANT EDITOR

Lesley Sudlow

ILLUSTRATOR

Jessica Stockham

COVER

Lynne Joesbury

SERIES DESIGNER

Sarah Rock

DESIGNER

Sarah Rock

AUTHOR

Jenni Tavener

To Alice Charlotte

Published by Scholastic Ltd,
Villiers House, Clarendon Avenue,
Leamington Spa, Warwickshire CV32 5PR

© 2000 Scholastic Ltd Text © 2000 Jenni Tavener
3 4 5 6 7 8 9   2 3 4 5 6 7 8 9

British Library Cataloguing-in-Publication Data
A catalogue record for this book is available from the British Library.

ISBN 0-439-01743-2

CONTENTS

INTRODUCTION

AUTUMN

TEACHERS' NOTES
PAGE 53

WINTER

TEACHERS' NOTES
PAGE 75

INTRODUCTION

Using themes

The theme of 'Seasons' can be used to help young children broaden their awareness of the world, and to become familiar with the changing weather conditions that continually follow an intriguing yearly cycle.

The *Themes for Early Years Photocopiables* series is designed to compliment the *Themes for Early Years* series. The activities in 'Seasons' build on ideas in four of the original titles: Spring, Summer, Autumn and Winter, and provide additional material to extend the theme. The book can be used in conjunction with the original series, but can equally well stand alone as an independent resource.

'Seasons' has four activity chapters each covering one of the four seasons. All of the activities are planned to support the QCA's Early Learning Goals, with each activity focusing on one of the six areas of learning: Personal, social and emotional development, Language and literacy, Mathematical development, Knowledge and understanding of the world, Physical development and Creative development.

The activities also offer opportunities for the children to experience important life skills such as working as a team, turn taking, decision making and voicing views and ideas.

How to use this book

The activity chapters within this book follow the same format, providing eighteen photocopiable activity sheets accompanied by four pages of activity notes.

The activity notes explain how to use each photocopiable sheet together with the learning objective of the activity and the recommended group size. Where appropriate, ideas are also given to simplify or extend the activity for younger or older, more able children.

Using photocopiables

Each photocopiable sheet is an individual activity that can be used on its own or as part of a topic on the seasons, or during a topic about the current season.

Many of the sheets, if enlarged on the photocopier, can be used in a different way. For example, the sheets designed to help pencil control, such as 'The scarecrow' on page 70 and 'Patterned scarves' on page 93, could be enlarged to A3 size and used with finger-paints instead of a pencil to encourage hand co-ordination skills for younger children.

The activities offer a wide variety of approaches to stimulate continued interest in the seasons theme. Some of the photocopiable sheets can be used by the children to create simple poems, for example 'Spring poem' on page 16 and 'Sunshine rhyme' on page 37.

Several of the photocopiable sheets can be turned into celebration cards, such as 'New Year's card' on page 90 and 'A 'cracking' card' on page 28, or mobiles, for example 'Candle bright' on page 67 and 'Rock-a-

bye baby' on page 60. Other sheets can be used as number games, keepsakes, booklets, puppets and to inspire action games.

'The four seasons' illustrations on pages 7 and 8 show how the scenery of a park changes according to the time of year and the weather conditions. These pictures can be used in a variety of ways:

• **Seasonal jigsaws**

Invite the children to colour in the pictures, then mount them onto card or laminate them. Help the children to cut each scene into four pieces to create a simple jigsaw.

• **Seasons poster**

Enlarge each picture to approximately A3 size. Invite the children to paint the scenes. Display them as colourful posters and use them to inspire discussion and observation skills.

• **Topic book covers**

For a topic on 'Spring' for example, make a copy of the spring picture for each child. Invite the children to use the picture to decorate the front cover of a 'topic book' or folder containing their own work about 'Spring'.

Using a wide variety of resources

Children enjoy the experience and stimulation of using different resources. All the resources required for the activities in this book are readily available in most early years settings or can be easily obtained, for example pens, paints, collage materials, scissors, glue, needle and thread and natural resources such as leaves, twigs and flowers.

Assessment and record-keeping

It is sometimes useful to collect and save a selection of each child's work during their early years at school or nursery to illustrate their ongoing achievements and/or to show evidence of the curriculum you have covered. Many of the photocopiable sheets in this book can be used for this purpose. Name and date copies of the completed sheets and, if appropriate, add extra information on the reverse. These sheets can then be stored in the children's personal files and used to show parents or new teachers when the need arises.

Home links

Establishing a link between home and school/nursery that is informative and friendly is extremely beneficial to all parties, especially the children. One way of initiating this link is to invite the parents or guardians to work with their child on an activity sent home by you, which is relevant to their child's current topic. Many of the photocopiable sheets in this book can be used for this purpose. Alternatively, the children could complete the activity at school/nursery and then take the resulting game, card, mobile or booklet for example, home to share with their family.

Spring

Summer

Autumn

Winter

SPRING

BEANSTALK HEIGHT CHART

PAGE 13

Learning objective
To inspire teamwork and co-operation to produce a height chart which can be used as a shared resource. (Personal, Social and Emotional Development)
Group size
Five children can create a chart 1m tall.

Provide each child with a copy of the photocopiable sheet. Explain that it represents one section of a beanstalk height chart.

Invite the children to decorate the leaves using crayons, paints, collage or a combination of all three techniques. When complete, help each child to cut across the top of their picture. Help them to glue or tape each section together to create one long beanstalk.

Write centimetre values (or use arbitrary units) along the side of the chart. Display on the wall and use as a shared resource for activities such as measuring and comparing heights.

Extend the activity by inviting the children to grow their own bean plants.

THE GIANT'S GARDEN

PAGE 14

Learning objective
To gain awareness about sharing and kindness. (Personal, Social and Emotional Development)
Group size
Small groups.

Read or tell the story *The Selfish Giant* by Oscar Wilde (Puffin), or use an adapted version.

The story is about a selfish giant who sent children away from his garden. The garden was so sad, that spring did not want to arrive. The garden stayed in winter for a long time. But one day, some children crept in the garden to play. The garden was so pleased to have children back, that spring arrived once more. The giant realized that he had been selfish and decided to start sharing his garden.

Give each child a copy of the photocopiable sheet showing the giant's winter garden. Invite them to turn the scene into a spring garden by adding birds, flowers, leaves, sun, grass, blossom, ducks on the pond, butterflies, bees and other insects, using crayons, pens or pencils.

Alternatively, provide each child with an enlarged sheet, and invite them to use painting equipment to change the scene.

CELEBRATION CARD

PAGE 15

Learning objective
To make and decorate a celebration card for someone special. (Personal, Social and Emotional Development)
Group size
Small groups or individuals.

There are many different events or customs which people celebrate during spring such as Valentine's Day, Easter Day, Mother's Day, Holi and Chinese New Year.

This photocopiable sheet can be easily adapted by the children to suit any of these occasions. Provide each child with a copy of the sheet to colour and decorate, using their own choice of media, for example pens, paints, collage or printing. Help them to cut around the black line and to stick their design onto folded card.

Encourage older children to 'have a go' at writing their own message inside the card. Scribe the words for younger children or let them copy a message in their own writing.

SPRING POEM

PAGE 16

Learning objective
To inspire an interest in poetic language. (Language and Literacy)
Group size
Small groups (or enlarge the photocopiable sheet to A3 size for a 'focus' activity for the whole group).

Prepare for this activity by taking the children outside to observe the season of spring and all that it brings from first-hand experience.

Give each child a copy of the photocopiable sheet and read the words of the poem to them. Encourage the children to write or draw on the lines three things that they have seen in spring. Provide a completed poem so that the children can see how the simple poem is formed. For example,

'Spring is here, and we can see... birds, flowers and butterflies ...for you and me'.

Alternatively, use the spring pictures on the photocopiable sheet to help

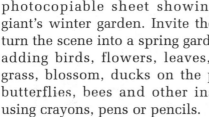

inspire ideas. Extend the activity for older children by asking them to elaborate on each word such as 'pretty birds', 'colourful flowers' and 'fluttering butterflies'.

PAGE 17
BABY ANIMALS

Learning objective
To develop an understanding of initial letter sounds and to help reading and writing skills. (Language and Literacy)
Group size
Small groups or individuals.

Give each child a copy of the photocopiable sheet. Read the words and say the initial letter sounds with each child. Encourage them to copy each word. Use this part of the activity to reinforce the correct way to write each letter. Invite the children to draw a line to match each name to the correct animal. Use this part of the activity to reinforce initial letter sounds and blends, for example 'c' for 'calf' and 'ch' for 'chick'. Extend the activity for older children by asking them to draw pictures of the adult animals on a separate sheet of paper, and to label them with the names: 'pig', 'cow', 'chicken' and 'sheep'.

PAGE 18
OLD MACDONALD'S NOISY FARM

Learning objective
To inspire reading and writing skills. (Language and Literacy)
Group size
Small groups to complete the photocopiable sheet; whole group to join in singing.

Sing the song, 'Old MacDonald had a Farm', including a piglet, calf, puppy and duckling. Encourage the children to identify and name the baby animals. Read the words in the speech bubbles to the children, and ask them to copy the words carefully. Invite the children to colour the animals, and to draw a line to match the correct sound to each baby animal.

PAGE 19
DOLLS' FESTIVAL GAME

Learning objective
To develop number identification and matching skills. (Mathematical Development)
Group size
A game for two players.

Provide each child with a copy of the photocopiable sheet, a crayon and a dice to share (showing dots, words or figures 1 to 6).

Tell the children how to play the game: the players should take turns to throw the dice and to colour in the matching dice on their photocopiable sheet. If the dice on the game sheet has already been coloured in, that player

misses a turn. The winner is the first player to colour in all six dice on their photocopiable sheet.

After the game, invite the children to use their imaginations to decorate the dolls' outfits. Use the activity to introduce the children to a festival celebrated in Japan on 3 March, called 'Dolls' Festival', when all girls are given a new doll.

PAGE 20
EGG HUNT

Learning objective
To encourage counting, pattern matching and number writing skills. (Mathematical Development)
Group size
Small groups.

Provide each child with a copy of the photocopiable sheet. Explain that 'egg hunting' is a popular tradition in Germany. Parents hide eggs in the garden for their children to find. Explain that there are two, three or four eggs of each pattern hidden in the picture. Challenge the children to find them and to write their answers in the appropriate boxes. When the children have found all the eggs, invite them to colour the picture. Enlarge the photocopiable sheet to A3 size for group work with younger children.

PAGE 21
SPRING PATCHWORK

Learning objective
To develop shape-matching skills and to inspire an awareness of tessellation. (Mathematical Development)
Group size
Small or large groups.

Provide each child with a copy of the photocopiable sheet. Encourage them to make up their own colour code, and to follow the code to decorate the shapes. Help them to cut out their finished flower picture.

Invite the children to glue their flower pictures together, patchwork style, onto a large sheet of paper or a display board.

Use the 'patchwork' to inspire an interest in tessellation. Provide shapes such as triangles or oblongs for the children to make up their own simple tessellating patterns.

PAGE 22
MY SEED PACKET

Learning objective
To develop an awareness of the link between seeds and flowers. (Knowledge and Understanding of the World)
Group size
Small groups.

Prepare for this activity by showing the children some seeds, such as sunflower seeds, and then showing them a sunflower plant, or pictures of a sunflower. Talk about how the seed grows into the plant.

Give each child a copy of the photocopiable sheet and show them how to cut, fold and glue it to make a small 'seed packet'. Encourage the children to trace the word 'seeds' and to draw a flower on the front of their packet. Ask them to write their name and the type of seeds that they have on the back of the packet.

Provide the children with seeds to save in their new packets until they are ready to plant them.

Alternatively, let the children take their seeds home for planting. (Check that the parents are 'willing and able' to do this before you send them home!)

PAGE 23
SPRING CREATURES

Learning objective
To develop observation and an awareness of the type of small creatures seen in spring. (Knowledge and Understanding of the World)
Group size
Small groups.

Provide each child with a copy of the photocopiable sheet. Encourage them to identify and draw a circle around the odd picture out in each row. Ask the children to explain why the picture is different to the others in that row.

Help the children to name the six different creatures (including the tadpole). If possible, organize a walk outside or through a park for the children to look for some of these creatures in their natural environment.

Invite the children to paint giant pictures of these small animals to create a lively 'Spring creatures' display, or a set of mobiles.

PAGE 24
WEATHER CHART

Provide each child with a copy of the photocopiable sheet, or display an A3 copy for the whole group to share. Invite the children to step outside with you, and encourage them to describe the type of weather that they can see and feel. Encourage them to record their findings by drawing a picture of the day's weather in the appropriate space on their sheet. Let them devise their own signs, symbols or pictures to represent different conditions such as 'sun', 'rain', 'wind' and so on. Repeat the activity every day for one week. At the end of the week, ask the children to give a little 'weather report', using their chart to help them explain what they saw each day.

Learning objective
To encourage observation and record-keeping skills. (Knowledge and Understanding of the World)
Group size
Individuals; small or large groups.

PAGE 25
CHINESE DRAGON PUPPET

Provide each child with a copy of the photocopiable sheet to colour in. Help them to cut around the lines to create the 'head' and 'tail' of a dragon. Provide strips of colourful fabric approximately 10cm x 30cm to represent the dragon's body, or invite the children to decorate their own strips of plain fabric using colourful fabric paints or thick felt-tipped pens.

Help the children to tape the fabric body between the paper head and tail and to tape two sticks, old rulers or pieces of dowelling onto each end of the dragon.

Invite the children to hold the sticks to manoeuvre their dragon puppet or to make it 'dance' to music. Use the puppet to inspire an interest in the Chinese New Year celebrations held each spring.

Learning objective
To help develop fine and gross motor skills (Physical Development)
Group size
Small groups.

PAGE 26
BABY BIRDS

Give each child a copy of the photocopiable sheet and invite them to colour in the pictures. Help them to cut out the three pictures, and to use a single-hole hole-punch to make two

Learning objective
To inspire manipulative skills (Physical Development)
Group size
Small groups.

holes in the large picture. Provide each child with a length of wool, approximately 30cm long, to thread through the holes. Help them to tape the parent birds onto the two loose ends of wool.

Show the children how to pull the wool to make one parent at a time take 'food' to the baby birds.

Use the activity to encourage an awareness of how parent animals care for their young.

PAGE 27
SPRING PICTURE FRAME

Prepare for this activity by taking the children outside to make observational drawings or to take photographs of a day in spring, for example new flowers, young animals, birds and butterflies. blossom or a sunny view.

Give each child a copy of the photocopiable sheet and encourage them to use coloured pens or pencils to follow the dotted lines. Help them to cut around the frame and to stick it onto card. Invite the children to stick their spring picture or photograph in the centre of the frame. Help them to tape a loop of thread to the back of the frame so it can be hung on the wall.

Arrange an exhibition of the children's pictures on a display board at the children's eye level.

PAGE 28
A 'CRACKING' CARD

Give each child a copy of the photocopiable sheet. Invite them to colour in the egg and to use their creative imaginations to draw an Easter theme picture in the centre. Ask the children to write who the card is to and from. Help each child to cut along the black line and to fold along the dotted

lines. When the card is closed, it shows a whole egg. When it is opened, the card reveals a cracked egg, a picture and the writing.

Invite older children to write an Easter greeting on the front or inside their card. Younger children could use finger-paints to create a speckly egg on the front and yellow sticky paper to make a chick inside their card.

PAGE 29
CAMOUFLAGE CATERPILLAR

Provide each child with a copy of the photocopiable sheet. Read the poem, and explain that some animals camouflage themselves by being the same colour as their surroundings, to stop other creatures preying on them. Encourage the children to use only blue and yellow paints to mix different shades of green for their caterpillar.

Provide each child with a leaf shape, approximately A4 size, and encourage them to paint it using similar shades of green.

When dry, help the children to cut out their caterpillar and mount it onto their leaf. Display the finished pictures on the wall, and encourage the children to view them from a distance to see the full camouflage effect.

PAGE 30
RANGOLI PATTERNS

Prepare for the activity by talking with the children about the festival of Holi (Festival of Colours) celebrated by Hindus in spring. Explain that Holi celebrates new beginnings and the end of winter, and is a time for having fun. Hindus often create colourful rangoli patterns outside their front doors. They use coloured spices, rice, chalk and sometimes powder paint to create the patterns. Show the children some examples of rangoli patterns in information books.

Provide each child with a copy of the photocopiable sheet. Invite them to use coloured pens, glitter, sequins, beads, lentils and other materials to create an original pattern on the 'doorstep'.

Beanstalk height chart

◆ Colour, paint or collage the beanstalk.

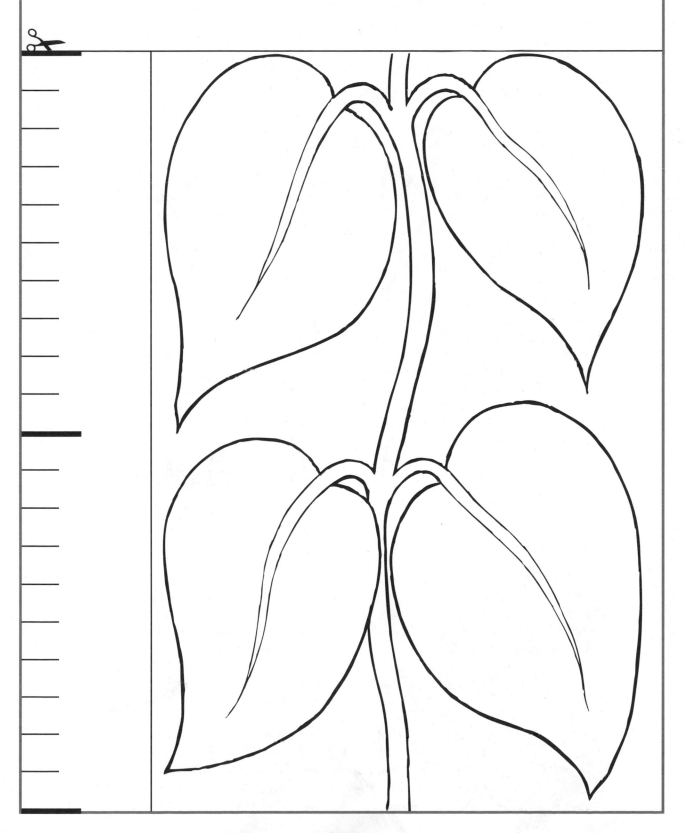

The giant's garden

◆ Turn this winter garden into a spring garden.

Celebration card

◆ Decorate, cut out and stick onto folded card.

Spring poem

◆ Write or draw three things that you can see in spring.

Spring is here,
and we can see...

_____

_____

and

_____

...for you and me.

Baby animals

◆ Write the words and match them to the correct animal.

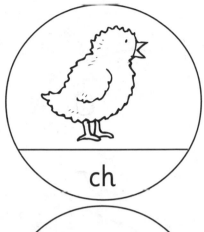

ch

c

l

p

c a l f

calf

c h i c k

_ _ _ _ _

p i g l e t

_ _ _ _ _ _

l a m b

_ _ _ _

Old MacDonald's noisy farm

◆ Copy the sounds made by the baby animals. Draw a line to match each sound to the four animals.

g r u n t

m o o

w o o f

q u a c k

Dolls' festival game

◆ You will need a dice and a crayon to play this game.

Egg hunt

◆ Count the eggs in the picture. Write your answers in the boxes.
How many?

Spring patchwork

◆ Make up your own colour code. Colour in and cut out your flower.

Colour code

My seed packet

◆ Make this special packet to put seeds in.

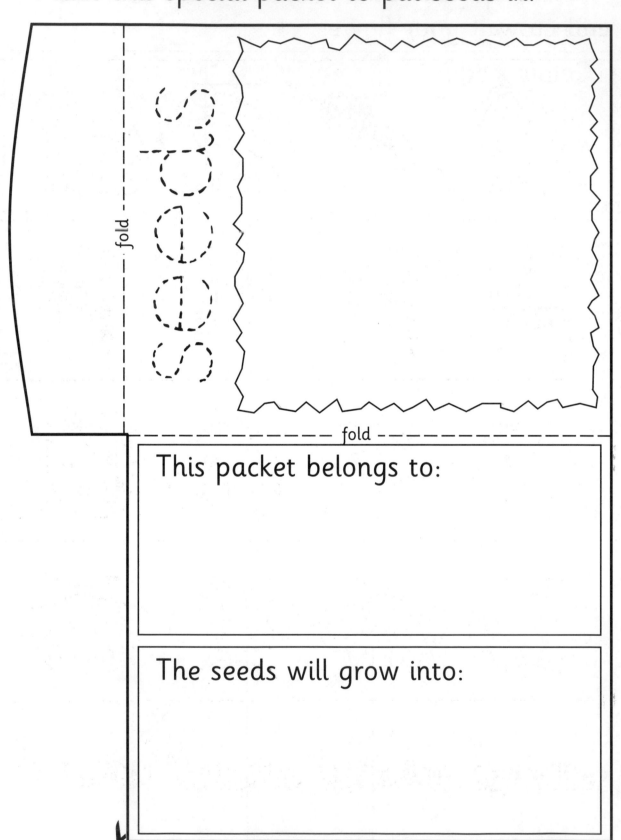

fold

seeds

fold

This packet belongs to:

The seeds will grow into:

Spring creatures

◆ Draw a circle around the odd one out in each row.

Weather chart

◆ Draw the type of weather that you can see.

Weather chart

Monday	Tuesday	Wednesday	Thursday	Friday

Chinese dragon puppet

◆ Colour or paint the head and tail of the dragon and cut them out.

Baby birds

◆ Colour in and cut out the pictures.

Spring picture frame

◆ Use coloured pens to follow the dotted lines.

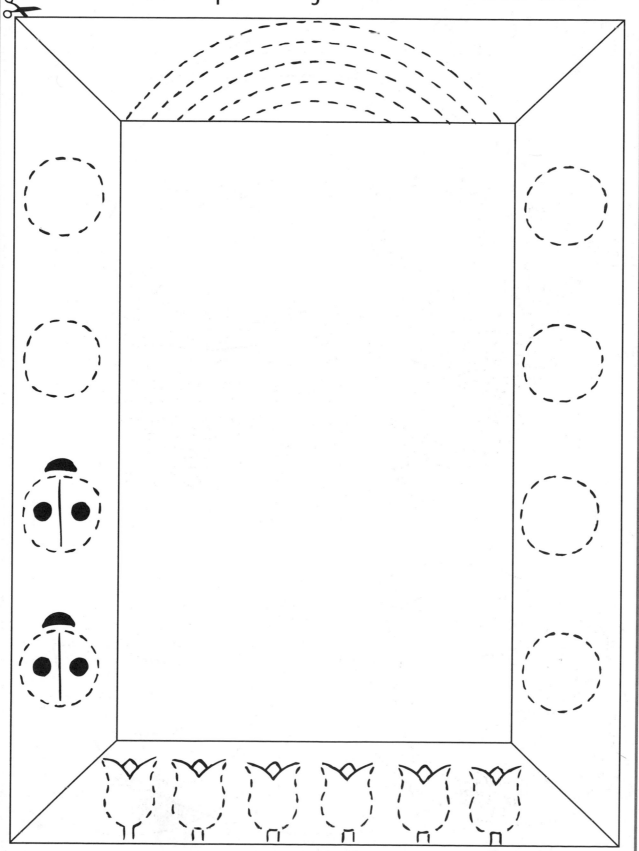

A 'cracking' card

◆ Draw a picture in the middle. Fold along
the dotted lines.

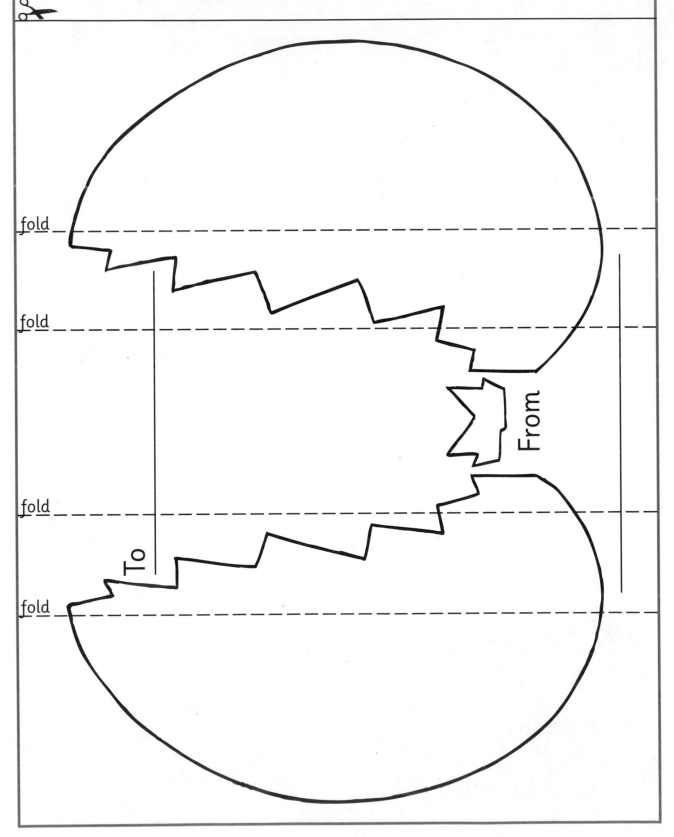

Camouflage caterpillar

◆ Mix blue and yellow together to paint the caterpillar in different shades of green.

A poem
Caterpillar long,
Caterpillar green,
Caterpillar in the
leaves,
hard to be seen!

Rangoli patterns

◆ Design a pattern on the doorstep.

SUMMER

PAGE 35
SUMMER MEMORIES

Learning
objective
To develop
fair play and
co-operation
and to
inspire home
links.
(Personal,
Social and
Emotional
Development)
Group size
A game for
two players.

Provide each child with two copies of the photocopiable sheet to colour in. Help them to stick the sheets onto thin card, and then to cut along the lines to produce twelve cards.

Encourage the children to use their set of cards to play games such as 'Snap' and 'Pairs'. Invite the children to take their game cards home to play with their friends and family to help establish or maintain home links.

PAGE 36
A SUMMER LOLLY

Learning
objective
To inspire
decision
making and
imagination.
(Personal,
Social and
Emotional
Development)
Group size
Individuals or
small groups.

Provide each child with a copy of the photocopiable sheet and a selection of coloured crayons, pens or pencils. Encourage the children to associate the different colours with flavours, for example, red for strawberry and yellow for banana. Alternatively, ask them to think of unusual flavours, such as red for tomato ketchup and yellow for cheese flavour.

Invite the children to select three colours to colour the lolly and to write the flavours in the panel. Scribe the words for younger children.

Display several summer lolly sheets together to create an ice-cream kiosk display in the role-play area.

PAGE 37
SUNSHINE RHYME

Provide each child with a copy of the photocopiable sheet. Read the unfinished rhyme. Ask the children to think of words to describe the sun and make a note of the words. Say the rhyme again, but this time include three of the children's words, for example, 'The sun is shining up so high... hot, bright, yellow ...in the sky'. Repeat the rhyme several times using a different selection of words. Invite the children to write three words, one in each 'sun' on their sheet, to create their own 'sunshine rhyme'.

Encourage older children to have a go at writing the words, and help younger children to 'copy write' or scribe the words for them. Secure several sheets together to form a sunshine rhyme book. Invite the children to design a cover for the book.

Learning
objective
To experience
writing a
simple rhyme.
(Language and
Literacy)
Group size
Small groups.

PAGE 38
HOT-AIR BALLOON

Show the children some pictures or photographs of real hot-air balloons, and ask them to identify the different colours. Give each child a photocopiable sheet and invite them to decorate the balloon by following the colour code. Encourage them to say the sounds out loud as they match each letter to the code.

Help younger children to colour in their code and encourage older children to read the colour words.

Cut out and glue the finished sheets back to back and hang them at varying heights to create colourful mobiles.

Learning
objective
To develop an
understanding
of initial letter
sounds.
(Language
and Literacy)
Group size
Small groups.

Learning objective
To encourage imagination and writing skills. (Language and Literacy).
Group size
Individuals or small groups.

PAGE 39
PICTURE POSTCARD

Provide each child with a copy of the photocopiable sheet and a collection of picture postcards showing scenery from real or imaginary places.

Encourage the children to look at the postcards to inspire their imagination about a 'dream' holiday destination. This could include a real place or somewhere imaginary such as Toyland or outer space.

Invite the children to draw a picture of their chosen destination on the blank postcard on their sheet. Help them to write who their postcard is to and from. Encourage older children to use the space at the bottom of the postcard to write a message. Younger children can fill the space with kisses or their surname.

Learning objective
To encourage reading and writing, and to reinforce initial letter sounds. (Language and Literacy)
Group size
Individuals or small groups.

PAGE 40
'S' FOR SEASIDE

Provide each child with a copy of the photocopiable sheet. Help the children look for, and say the sounds: 's', 'sk', 'sh' and 'sp'.

Encourage the children to match the six words in the boxes to the pictures in the seaside scene. Help them to write the words in the correct places. Let the children colour in the picture.

Encourage older children to identify objects around the room which begin with the same sounds.

Learning objective
To encourage number matching and number recognition skills. (Mathematical Development)
Group size
Individuals or small groups.

PAGE 41
PRETTY PETALS

Provide each child with a copy of the photocopiable sheet. Encourage them to use five different colours to complete the colour code at the top of the sheet, then ask them to follow their code to decorate the flower petals.

Let the group assemble a shared display by cutting out their flowers and gluing them randomly onto a background of green paper.

Invite the children to make potato print butterflies. Help them to cut out and hang the prints in front of their display to create a 3-D effect.

PAGE 42
BEE GAME

Provide each child with a copy of the photocopiable sheet. Encourage them to write over the dotted lines to form the numbers 1 to 10.

Give each child a counter and provide a dice to share. The players should place their counter on 'Start' and take tuns to throw the dice and move accordingly along the flowers.

If a player lands on a flower occupied by a bee they must go back to the start. The winner is the first player to reach the flower marked 'Finish'.

Extend the activity for older children by inviting them to write rules and instructions for the game, and to make counters to resemble bees.

Learning objective
To inspire number writing skills and an interest in playing number games. (Mathematical Development)
Group size
A game for two players.

PAGE 43
SUMMER FRUITS

Provide each child with a copy of the photocopiable sheet. Talk about the positioning of the fruit using words such as 'in front', 'behind', 'upside-down', 'above', 'below' and 'beside'.

Encourage the children to draw a circle around the 'odd one out' in each row. Ask them to explain why they think that picture is different to the rest. Extend the activity by inviting the children to arrange some real fruit (or play fruit) by listening to and following instructions such as 'put the apple behind the pear' or 'place the banana in front of the orange'.

Learning objective
To develop skills in problem solving and following instructions. (Mathematical Development)
Group size
Small groups.

PAGE 44

THERE'S SUNSHINE

Learning objective
To encourage thought and reflection about the beauty of a summer's day. (Knowledge and Understanding of the World)
Group size
Whole group.

Display an enlarged copy of the photocopiable sheet where it can be seen easily by all of the children. Say the rhyme, 'There's sunshine':
There's sunshine on my ice-cream,
There's sunshine in the air,
There's sunshine on my glasses,
There's sunshine in my hair,
There's sunshine in the water,
There's sunshine on my chair,
There's sunshine all around me,
There's sunshine everywhere.

Encourage the children to join in with the words to the rhyme using the pictures on the sheet to help them. Use the rhyme to initiate discussion about the things that the children like to do on a summer's day. Invite older children to create a 'mini-rhyme booklet' by cutting a copy of the sheet into eight separate pictures and securing them together in the correct order. Help them to add a front cover showing the words, 'There's sunshine'.

PAGE 45

FLOWER HUNT

Learning objective
To encourage an interest in nature and to develop observation skills. (Knowledge and Understanding of the World)
Group size
Small groups. (Arrange for extra supervision during the flower hunt outside.)

Take the children to a safe place outside where they can participate in a flower hunt to collect daisies, buttercups, clover and dandelions.

Back indoors, provide each child with a copy of the photocopiable sheet. Invite them to identify, name and match the four flowers that they have collected to the pictures on their sheet. Help the children to tape the flowers onto the sheet in the first column, and to use close observation to draw a picture of each flower in the remaining spaces. Alternatively, press each flower before taping it onto the sheet.

Use the activity for older children to inspire an interest in nature books. Organize a trip to a library to observe the wide variety of books available.

PAGE 46

WEAVE A NEST

Learning objective
To develop dexterity and manipulative skills. (Physical Development)
Group size
Small groups.

Help the children to prepare for the activity by cutting out and gluing their photocopiable sheets onto card. An adult should then use a hole-punch to pierce the eight holes around the nest.

Invite the children to weave a length of thick brown thread, such as wool, through the holes in random order. Help them to secure the loose ends of their thread to the back of the picture.

Encourage the children to repeat this process several times using different shades of brown thread, until their picture resembles a tangled birds' nest.

Display several nests together on a green background and cut to resemble a bush or treetop. Use the display to inspire mathematical language such as, 'How many nests?', 'Count the number of birds in each nest', 'Which nest is up high?', 'Find the nest with the most/ least birds'.

PAGE 47

T-SHIRT DESIGNS

Learning objective
To develop pencil control and to practise writing patterns. (Physical Development)
Group size
Individuals or small groups.

Provide each child with a copy of the photocopiable sheet and a selection of sharp, coloured pencils. Encourage them to decorate the T-shirt by following the dotted lines carefully, in the direction of the arrows.

Use the activity to inspire discussion about wearing hats, T-shirts and sun cream when playing out in the hot sun.

PAGE 48

MY SPOTTY KITE

Learning objective
To inspire fine and gross motor skills. (Physical Development)
Group size
Individuals or small groups.

Provide each child with a copy of the photocopiable sheet, coloured paints and a selection of thick and thin paintbrushes. Invite the children to carefully paint the spots on the kite. When the paintings are dry, help the children to cut around the kite shape and to attach a length of thick wool or ribbon to create a tail.

When the kites are complete, take the children to a place outside where they can move around freely and safely. Invite the children to run about and fly their kites.

Extend the activity for older children by inviting them to decorate their kite's tail with knots of coloured ribbon.

PAGE 49
SUMMER GARDEN

Learning objective
To inspire an enthusiasm for mixing primary colours. (Creative Development)
Group size
Individuals or small groups.

Give each child a copy of the photocopiable sheet, paints in the three primary colours – red, blue and yellow – and painting equipment.

Show the children how to mix the paints to create secondary colours, for example red and yellow to make orange, blue and yellow to make green, blue and red to make purple. Encourage the children to use the colours that they have mixed to paint the flowers on their sheet.

Provide younger children with an enlarged copy of the sheet to paint. Extend the activity for older children by providing fine paintbrushes to add extra detail. When complete, mount several pictures together to create a summer garden display.

PAGE 50
PRESSED FLOWERS

Learning objective
To have first-hand experience of a traditional craft and to create an original picture. (Creative Development)
Group size
Small groups.

If possible, prepare well in advance for this activity by helping the children to grow their own flowers from seeds, following the instructions on the packet. Alternatively, use fresh 'cut flowers'. Invite the children to press their flowers using a traditional flower press or by placing the flowers between sheets of blotting paper and weighing them down under some heavy books.

Leave the flowers to press for approximately one week, then help the children to arrange and glue their pressed flowers inside the oval on their sheet. Encourage them to write their name underneath. Invite older children to mount their work onto folded card and to write a message inside for someone special.

PAGE 51
THE SUN HAS GOT HIS HAT ON!

Sing the song, 'The sun has got his hat on' with the children (see below). Provide each child with a copy of the photocopiable sheet and a range of resources for colouring and drawing such as crayons, pencils, pastels or felt-tipped pens.

Invite the children to colour the sun and to design him a hat. Encourage older children to draw a few draft ideas on rough paper first, and then to select the one they like best to draw on their sheet. Provide younger children with an enlarged copy of the sheet and a selection of coloured paints, to create a bold, bright sunhat.

Display all the pictures on the wall with the words of the song:

The sun has got his hat on, hip hip hip hooray,
The sun has got his hat on and he's coming out to play.

Learning objective
To initiate an interest in simple design and to inspire learning a 'new' song. (Creative Development)
Group size
Individuals or small groups.

PAGE 52
SUMMER PARASOL

Provide each child with a copy of the photocopiable sheet, glue and a range of collage materials cut into small pieces such as shiny paper, fabric, wool, sequins, patterned paper, lace and ribbon.

Invite the children to use the various collage materials to decorate the parasol. Encourage older children to use the different colours or textures to create patterns. Help younger children by enlarging the sheet for paired or group work.

Learning objective
To develop creative imagination and to encourage an interest in collage. (Creative Development)
Group size
Small groups.

Summer memories

◆ Colour in the pictures and cut them out.

A summer lolly

◆ Choose three colours for your lolly. Write down the three flavours.

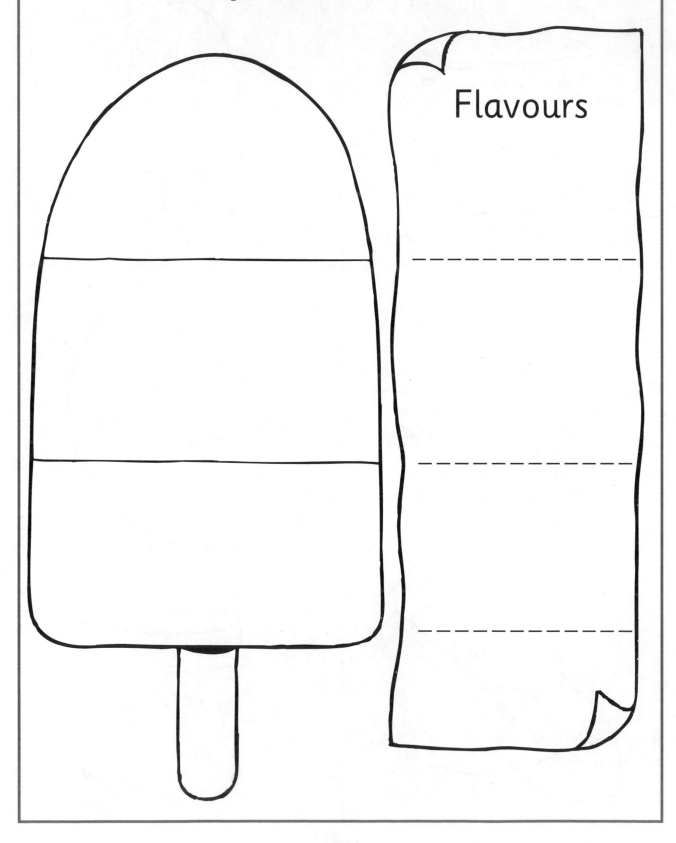

Flavours

_____

_____

_____

Sunshine rhyme

◆ Write three words to describe the sun.

The sun is shining up so high...

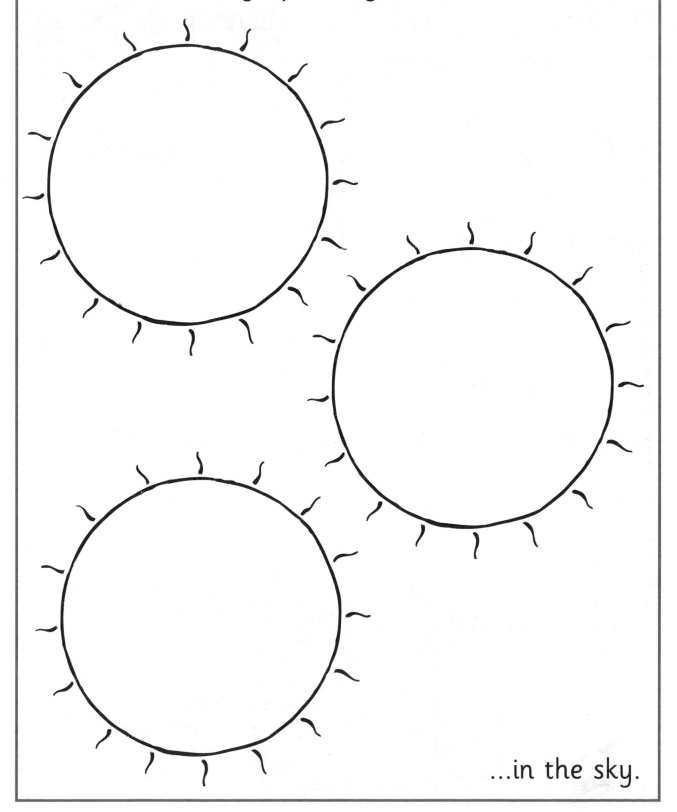

...in the sky.

Hot-air balloon

◆ Follow the code to colour in the balloon.

Colour code

g | green   r | red   b | blue   y | yellow

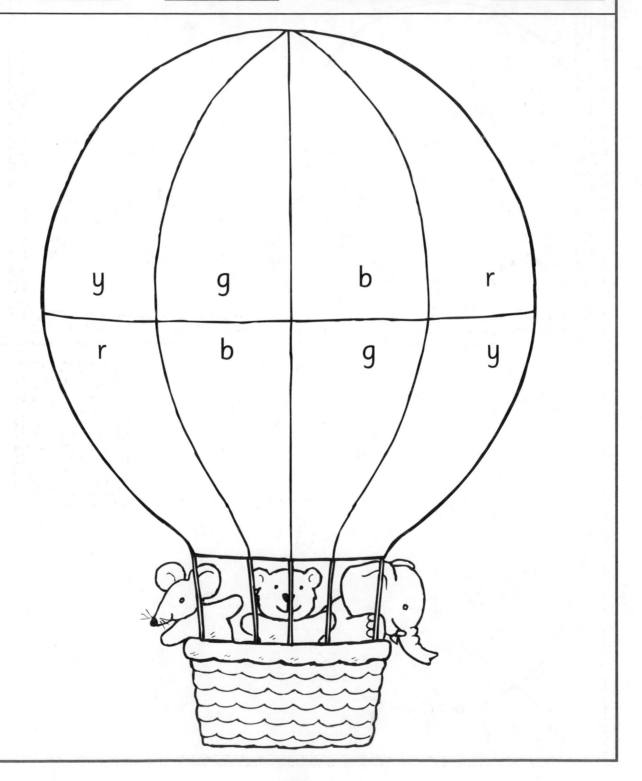

Picture postcard

◆ Draw a picture and write your message.

To _____

From _____

10P

'S' for seaside

◆ Write the 's' words in the correct places.
Colour the scene.

sun	sea	sand
sky	ship	spade

s h ___ ___ ___

s ___ ___ ___

s ___ ___ ___

s p ___ ___ ___ ___

s ___ ___ ___ ___

Pretty petals

◆ Make up your own colour code. Follow your code to decorate the flower.

Colour code

 1    2   3   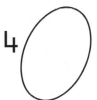 4    5

4

2

1

5

3

Bee game

◆ Write the numbers. Use a dice and counters to play this game.

Summer fruits

◆ Draw a circle around the odd one out in each row.

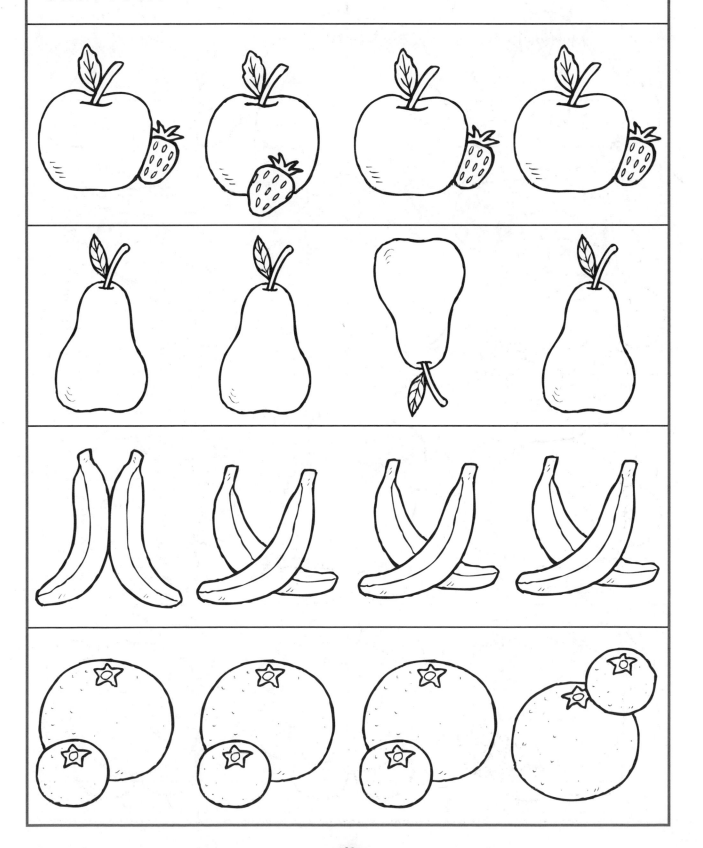

There's sunshine

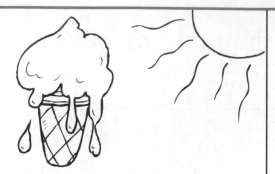

on my ice-cream

in the air

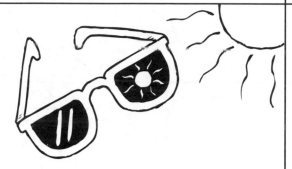

on my glasses

in my hair

in the water

on my chair

all around me

everywhere.

Flower hunt

◆ Find the four flowers. Use one space for the real flower and draw your own picture in the other space.

daisy		
buttercup		
clover		
dandelion		

Weave a nest

◆ Cut out and stick onto card. Draw some birds in the nest.

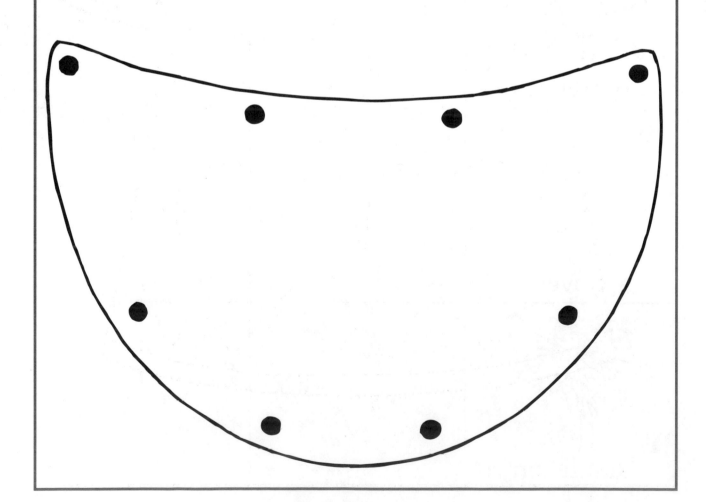

T-shirt designs

◆ Start at the dots and follow the arrows.

My spotty kite

◆ Use thick and thin paintbrushes to paint the spots.

Summer garden

◆ Mix up your own colours to paint the flowers.

Pressed flowers

◆ Glue some pressed flowers in the oval.

To _____

From _____

The sun has got his hat on!

◆ Colour in the sun and design a hat.

Summer parasol

◆ Use colourful collage to decorate the parasol.

AUTUMN

PAGE 57

APPLE HARVEST GAME

Learning objective
To promote turn taking and co-operation. (Personal, Social and Emotional Development)
Group size
A game for two to three players.

Provide each child with a copy of the photocopiable sheet together with a red, green and yellow crayon. Invite them to help make a coloured dice by placing two red, two green and two yellow sticky labels onto the faces of an old wooden brick.

Tell the children how to play the game. The players should take turns to throw the dice and to colour in one apple on their sheet by following the code. If they throw a colour, say red, and all the red apples on their sheet have been coloured in, then they should pass the dice to the next player. The winner is the first player to colour in all nine apples on their sheet.

PAGE 58

NIGHT DRAWS IN

Learning objective
To inspire imagination and self-confidence. (Personal, Social and Emotional Development)
Group size
Small groups.

Give each child a copy of the photocopiable sheet. Explain that the picture shows a child who has been tucked up in bed and is thinking of all their favourite things to help them get to sleep. Invite each child to think about their own favourite things such as toys, people, food or games, and to draw pictures of these things in the space. Sing the song or listen to a tape of 'My Favourite Things' from *The Sound of Music*.

PAGE 59

FIREWORK NIGHT

Learning objective
To promote an awareness of animal welfare on firework night. (Personal, Social and Emotional Development)
Group size
Small groups.

Have a general discussion with the children about what happens around 5 November. Encourage them to think about how animals might feel while fireworks are whizzing and banging in the sky. Explain that pets often get frightened by the loud noises and strange sights, and feel safer indoors.

Provide each child with a copy of the photocopiable sheet. Ask them to draw one or more pets safe inside the house, and to fill the sky with drawings of colourful fireworks.

PAGE 60

ROCK-A-BYE BABY

Learning objective
To inspire an interest in a traditional rhyme. (Language and Literacy)
Group size
Small groups.

Sing or say the rhyme 'Rock-a-bye Baby' with the children. Provide each child with a copy of the photocopiable sheet and encourage them to colour in and cut out the picture. Punch a hole in the top of their picture and help them to thread a loop of wool or ribbon (approximately 20cm) through the hole. Give each child a cardboard tube to represent a bough. Invite them to cut out and attach paper leaves to the tube using autumn colours. Let the children hang their baby picture from their bough and to blow like the wind to make the baby rock.

Create an unusual 3-D display by attaching the boughs to the top of a tree (approximately 1–2m tall) cut from coloured paper and mounted onto the wall or a display board. Attach the words to the rhyme on the trunk to inspire reading skills.

THE ENORMOUS TURNIP (PARTS 1 AND 2)

Learning objective
To initiate story-telling skills. (Language and Literacy)
Group size
Individuals or small groups.

Read the traditional story 'The Enormous Turnip' (Ladybird) to the children. Provide each child with a copy of both photocopiable sheets (Parts 1 and 2), to colour in and cut out. Help them to arrange the eight pictures in order and to retell the story using the pictures and captions as a guide. Invite older children to make a zigzag book using the pictures. Help younger children to stick the pictures in sequence onto a large sheet of card to create a storyboard.

PAGE 63

FRUIT AND VEGETABLES

Learning objective
To help distinguish letter sounds which are similar and to gain an awareness of harvest festival traditions. (Language and Literacy)
Group size
Individuals or small groups.

Provide each child with a copy of the photocopiable sheet. Explain that the picture represents fruit and vegetables displayed for a harvest festival celebration. Ask the children to write 'f' for fruit and 'v' for vegetable in the appropriate boxes. Help will probably be needed for some items. A tomato, for example, is actually a 'fruit' because it is the seed-containing part of a plant. Younger children may need practice at sounding out 'v' and 'f' as they can be easily confused. Older children could extend the activity by helping to arrange a real harvest festival display.

PAGE 64

THE ACORN HUNT

Learning objective
To develop counting and problem-solving skills. (Mathematical Development)
Group size
Individuals or small groups.

Give each child a copy of the photocopiable sheet. Ask them to count the acorns along each pathway and to write the answers on the tree stumps. Use the photocopiable sheet to inspire simple problem-solving skills by asking questions such as, 'Which squirrel will find the most acorns?', 'Which squirrel will find the least acorns?', 'How many acorns will the third squirrel find?'. Ask older children questions such as, 'Are the numbers on the sheet odd or even?', 'Can you count up to ten in twos?', 'Can you write a list of odd numbers between 1 and 10?'.

PAGE 65

AUTUMN LEAVES

Provide each child with a copy of the photocopiable sheet and three colours – red, brown and yellow. Ask them to colour the leaves using these colours. When every leaf is coloured in, ask the children to count how many leaves of each colour are in their picture and to write their answers in the appropriate boxes. Mount several sheets on a display board and invite older children to observe how many different variations were achieved by one group of children. Alternatively, they could find out if any of the sheets show the same answers.

Learning objective
To develop counting and recording skills. (Mathematical Development)
Group size
Small groups.

PAGE 66

WASHING IN THE WIND

Give each child a copy of the photocopiable sheet and a pencil. Encourage them to draw matching patterns on each pair of mittens, gloves and socks. Help younger children by inviting them to practice sorting and matching a set of real gloves and mittens. Extend the activity for older children by inviting them to draw matching coloured patterns on the socks, mittens and gloves.

Learning objective
To encourage matching and sorting skills. (Mathematical Development)
Group size
Individuals or small groups.

PAGE 67
CANDLE BRIGHT

Learning objective
To develop an awareness of the different forms of lighting we use now, compared to the past. (Knowledge and Understanding of the World)
Group size
Small groups.

Provide each child with a copy of the photocopiable sheet together with a white wax crayon (or candle) and encourage them to decorate the candle shapes. Ask the children to press down firmly as they draw with the crayon or candle. Invite the children to gently paint over the top of their design using watered-down paint. The paint will not cover the wax, so their decoration will 'magically' appear.

When dry, help the children to cut, fold and glue their sheet to create a double-sided candle mobile. Use the mobiles to inspire awareness that in autumn it begins to get dark early and that people who lived in the past had to rely on candlelight.

PAGE 68
APPLE PRINTS

Learning objective
To develop an awareness that apple trees grow from apple pips. (Knowledge and Understanding of the World)
Group size
Small groups.

Give each child a copy of the photocopiable sheet, apples cut in half and shallow trays of colourful paint for printing. Invite the children to fill the apple shape on their sheet with apple prints. The prints can be spaced out or overlapping. When dry, help the children to cut around the outer line. Mount two pictures back to back and add a thread through the hole in the stalk to create an apple-print mobile.

During the activity, encourage the children to find and observe the pips in their cut apples. Talk about how apple trees grow from apple pips. Follow up the activity by inviting the children to plant some pips to see if they grow.

PAGE 69
THE FALL

Provide each child with a copy of the photocopiable sheet and a selection of finger-paints in autumn shades such as red, orange, brown and yellow. Invite the children to fill the page with fingerprints to represent autumn leaves on the tree and falling to the ground. Use the activity to introduce the terms 'evergreen' and 'deciduous'. Explain that 'evergreen' plants and trees keep green leaves all year round, but 'deciduous' trees lose their leaves every autumn and grow new leaves in spring.

Learning objective
To inspire an understanding of the term 'deciduous trees' (Knowledge and Understanding of the World)
Group size
Individuals or small groups.

PAGE 70
THE SCARECROW

Provide each child with a copy of the photocopiable sheet and sharp coloured pencils. Encourage them to decorate the scarecrow by following the shapes and patterns in the direction of the arrows. Simplify the activity for younger children by providing an A3 copy of the sheet and a selection of thick crayons or finger-paints to follow the patterns.

Learning objective
To develop hand control and pre-writing skills. (Physical Development)
Group size
Individuals or small groups.

PAGE 71
MIGRATING BIRDS

Learning objective
To develop fine and gross motor skills. (Physical Development)
Group size
Small groups.

Provide each child with a copy of the photocopiable sheet and invite them to colour in the bird picture. Help each child to measure a length of card to fit around their head. Help them to cut around the outer line, and to glue or tape the centre of the bird to their headband. Invite the children to wear their head-dress as they mime the actions of a bird in flight. As the children move around and change direction, the 'wings' on their head-dress will 'flap' back and forth in the breeze. Use the activity to inspire an interest in 'migration'.

Extend the activity by inviting the children to wear their head-dresses for an action rhyme. Encourage them to stand in a circle (not holding hands) and to sing the following song and to do the accompanying actions. The song is an adaptation of 'In and Out the Dusty Bluebells'.

In and out the flock of birds (x 3)
(The first child (the leader) weaves between the circle of children, pretending to fly.)
You shall be my partner.
(The leader stops behind one child in the circle.)
Flap, flap, flap, flap, on your shoulder (x 3)
(The leader gently pats the child on their shoulder.)
You shall be my partner.
(This child now follows the leader as they both weave between the circle of children.)

Repeat the actions until all the children are following the leader and none are left in the circle. Invite them to 'fly' around as if they are a flock of birds flying home.

PAGE 72
SQUIRREL COLLAGE

Give each child a copy of the photocopiable sheet, some fabric glue and a selection of fabric swatches in shades of greys, reds, browns and oranges. Invite the children to glue the swatches onto their squirrel picture. Provide beads or buttons for the eye and nose and card ovals for the acorn. Help the children to cut around their collage. Mount several squirrels on a display board covered in green fabric, shaped to resemble a treetop. Staple some scrunched-up paper behind the green fabric to create a 3-D effect.

Challenge older children to cut out oak leaf shapes to add to the display. Provide younger children with an enlarged copy of the sheet to make a group collage.

Learning objective
To experience creating a fabric collage. (Creative Development)
Group size
Small groups.

PAGE 73
HANDPRINT HEDGEHOG

Provide each child with a copy of the photocopiable sheet, a tray of brown paint and an apron. You will also need hand-washing facilities nearby. Invite the children to give the hedgehog a coat of handprint 'prickles' using the brown paint. Use the activity to inspire the children's interest in animals that hibernate. Keep some reference and picture books nearby to help the children's curiosity. Encourage them to identify as many animals as possible that hibernate.

Learning objective
To inspire an interest in hibernation. (Creative Development)
Group size
Individuals or small groups.

PAGE 74
AUTUMN SHADES

Provide each child with a copy of the photocopiable sheet, painting equipment and powder paints in red and yellow only. Invite the children to mix the two colours to create a different shade of orange for each leaf. Invite older children to use all three primary colours – red, yellow and blue – to create a different shade of brown for each leaf. Invite the children to cut out their pictures and to arrange several sheets together to create a colourful autumn display.

Learning objective
To encourage an understanding of how to create shades of one colour. (Creative Development)
Group size
Individuals or small groups.

Apple harvest game

◆ Use red, green and yellow crayons and a coloured dice to play.

r red   g green   y yellow

Night draws in

◆ Draw pictures of your favourite things.

Firework night

◆ Draw some pets safely inside the house. Draw colourful fireworks in the sky.

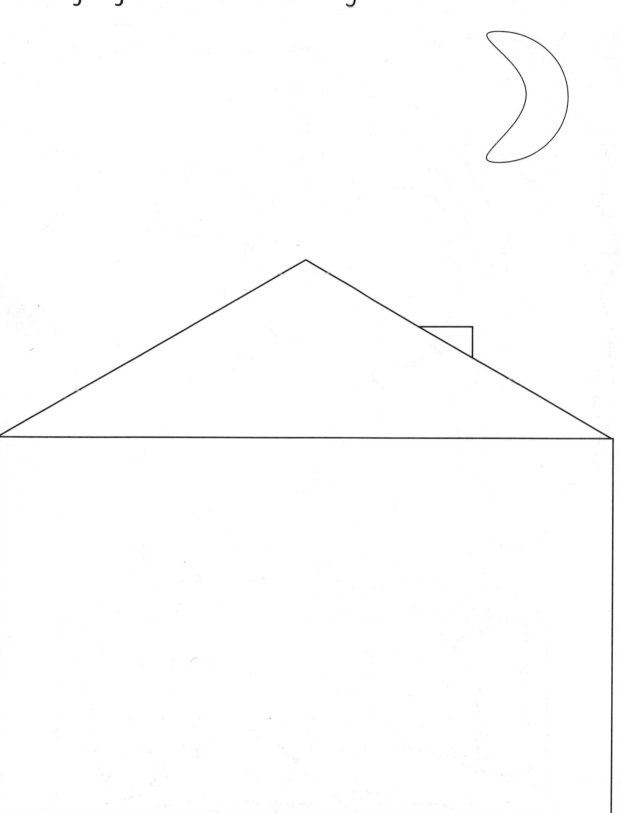

Rock-a-bye baby

◆ Colour in and cut out the picture.

The enormous turnip (Part 1)

◆ Colour the pictures, cut them out and put them in the correct order. Retell the story.

The woman helped.	The girl helped.

The boy helped.	**The man pulled.**

The enormous turnip (Part 2)

◆ Colour the pictures, cut them out and put them in the correct order. Retell the story.

The dog helped.	The cat helped.
	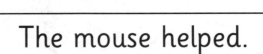
They all fell over.	The mouse helped.

Fruit and vegetables

◆ Write 'f' for fruit. Write 'v' for vegetables.

The acorn hunt

◆ Which squirrel will find the most acorns on his path?

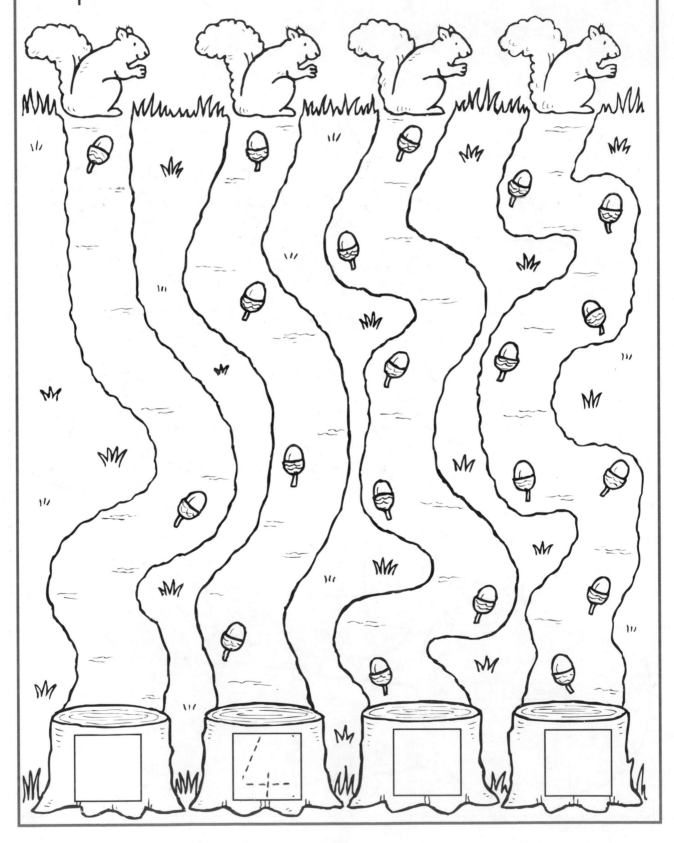

Autumn leaves

◆ Colour the leaves red, brown and yellow.

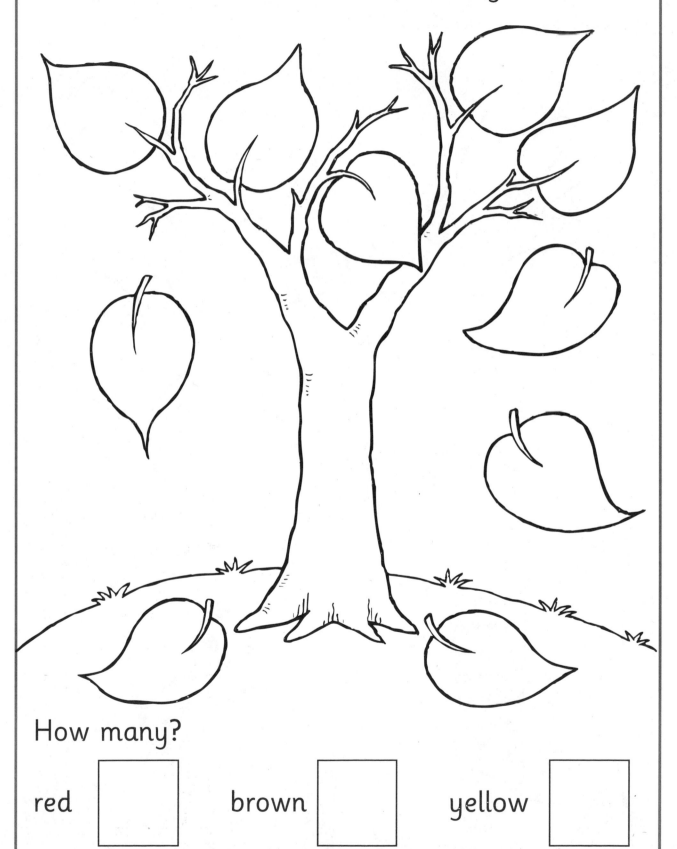

How many?

red [ ]   brown [ ]   yellow [ ]

Washing in the wind

◆ Draw matching patterns on each pair of mittens, gloves and socks.

Candle bright

◆ Decorate both sides of the candle.

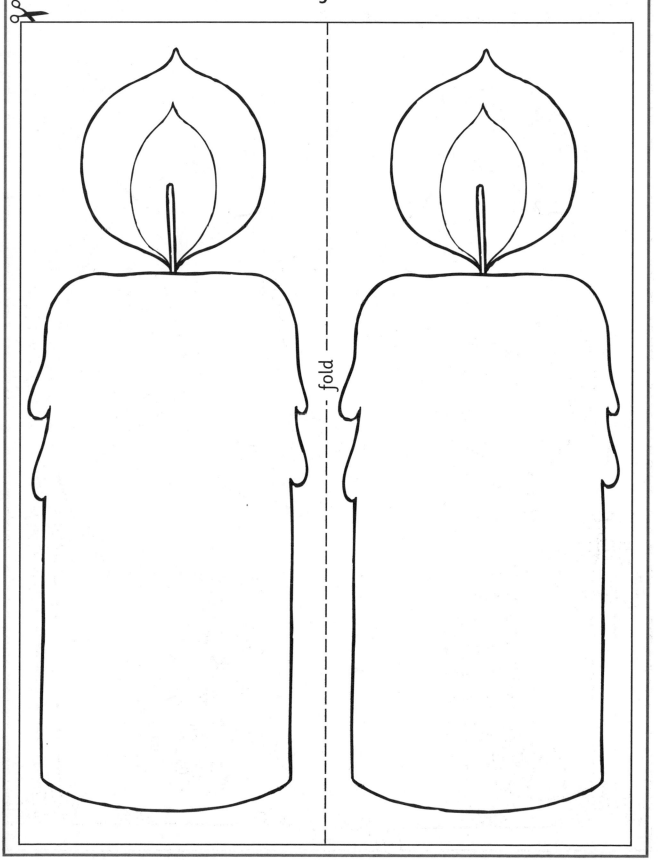

fold

Apple prints

◆ Fill the shape with colourful apple prints.

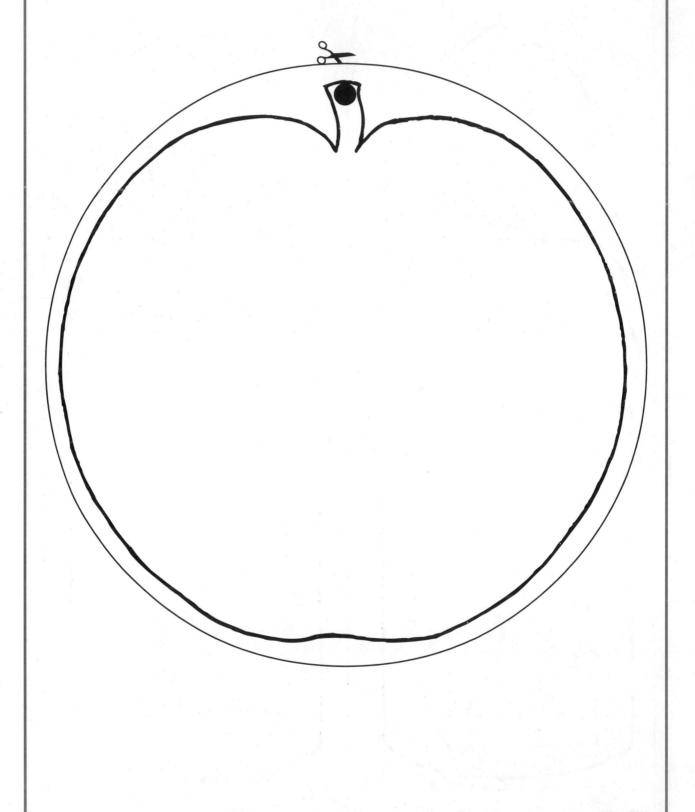

The fall

◆ Fill the page with fingerprint leaves.

The scarecrow

◆ Use coloured pens and pencils to decorate the scarecrow.

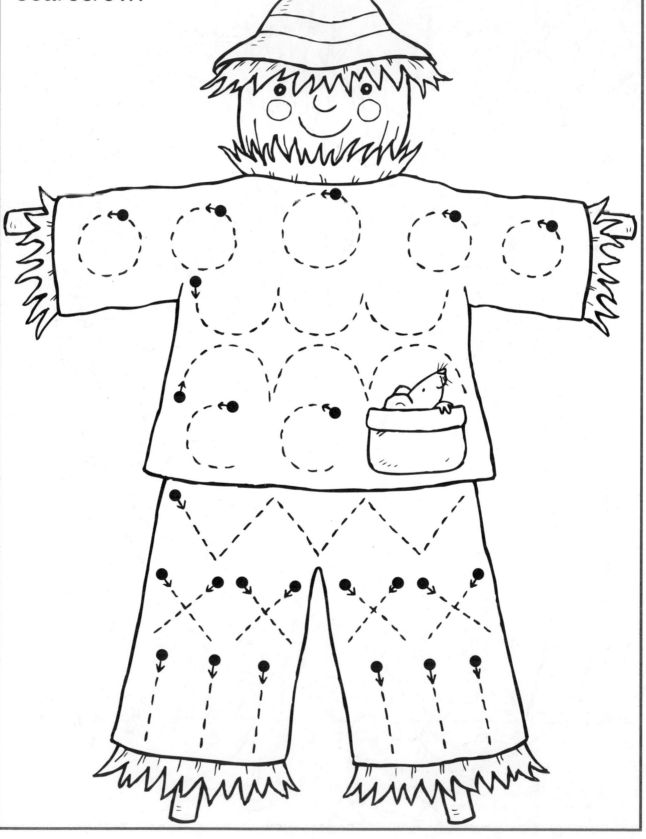

Migrating birds

◆ Colour in the bird picture, then cut around the outer line and glue the bird to a card headband.

Squirrel collage

◆ Choose some fabric to decorate the squirrel and then cut it out.

Handprint hedgehog

◆ Give the hedgehog a 'coat' of handprint prickles.

Autumn shades

◆ Mix your own autumn colours to paint these leaves.

WINTER

PAGE 79
VALENTINE HEART

Give each child a copy of the photocopiable sheet and encourage them to decorate the heart shape using coloured pens or paints. Provide an assortment of small collage materials such as ribbons, lace, bows, sequins, buttons and so on for added detail.

Invite older children to write who their Valentine heart is to and from and help younger children to copy write or scribe the words for them.

When complete, invite the children to cut out and stick their design onto coloured card. Use a hole-punch where indicated on the sheet, then help the children to thread ribbon through the holes and tie a decorative bow.

Use the activity to inspire discussion about people the children care about.

PAGE 80
WINTER BIRDS

Give each child a copy of the photocopiable sheet. Take the children to a place indoors where they can easily view birds through a window. Encourage birds by placing food and water nearby. Invite the children to record their observations on their sheet by writing or drawing where they saw each bird, for example on the grass or on a bird table. If different birds appear, help the children to draw pictures of them on a separate sheet of paper.

Cut out and secure several sheets together to form a 'Winter Birds' book. Use the activity to inspire discussion about the needs of birds in winter.

PAGE 81
KEEPING WARM

Provide each child with a copy of the photocopiable sheet. Help them to cut out the four pictures and encourage them to arrange the pictures in order to show the child either putting on or taking off his coat.

Use the activity to inspire discussion about clothing for different seasons and weather conditions. Inspire the children by asking funny questions such as, 'Would the child need this coat in the sun?', 'Would the child wear flip-flops in the snow?', 'Would they wear swimming trunks in a thunderstorm?'.

Follow up the activity by inviting the children to paint pictures of people in different items of warm clothing for a winter scene display.

PAGE 82
A WINTER'S DAY

Take the children outside on a winter's day. Encourage them to talk about what they can see, hear and feel.

Back indoors, give each child a copy of the photocopiable sheet. Help them to recall and then write the words and phrases that they used to describe the winter's day. Encourage older children to have a go at writing the words and help younger children to form their letters correctly as they copy write. Cut out and secure several sheets together and add a cover to create a group book titled 'A winter's day'.

PAGE 83
SNOWMAN STORY

Learning objective
To inspire discussion about a popular story. (Language and Literacy)
Group size
Individuals or small groups.

Read the story *The Snowman* by Raymond Briggs (Puffin). Give each child a copy of the photocopiable sheet. Invite them to draw the snowman at night, under the moon, and the melted snowman in the morning, under the sun. Help the children to cut out two rectangles of fabric (measuring approximately 15cm by 20cm) to glue above each window to represent curtains. Invite the children to use their pictures to inspire discussion about what happened in the story. Display the pictures on the wall at the children's own height with a title such as 'Melting snowmen'.

Encourage older children to draw or write about other favourite scenes from the story to include in the display.

PAGE 84
CHILLY WORDS

Learning objective
To encourage descriptive language and to inspire an interest in reading and writing. (Language and Literacy)
Group size
Small groups.

Talk with the children about what it feels like to be outside in the snow. Encourage them to think of different words to describe the weather such as white, icy and freezing.

Give each child a copy of the photocopiable sheet and invite them to choose three descriptive words to write onto their snowflake. Let older children have a go at writing the words. Help younger children to form their letters correctly as they copy write.

Extend the activity by helping the children to cut out and stick their snowflake onto a circle of card. Loosely secure the snowflake onto a second, slightly larger circle of card using a split-pin fastener.

Display the spinning snowflakes at the children's height to inspire an interest in reading new words.

PAGE 85
HOLLY AND IVY GAME

Learning objective
To encourage counting on and counting back. (Mathematical Development)
Group size
A game for two players.

Provide each child with a copy of the photocopiable sheet. Ask them to write the numbers 1 to 10 by following the dotted lines. Let them colour the holly berries in red and the leaves in green, using coloured pencils.

Tell the children how to play the game. Give each child a counter, and provide a dice to share. The players should place their counters on 'Start' and take turns to throw the dice and to move accordingly along the leaves. If a player lands on a prickly holly leaf, clearly identified by its red berries, they must move back one space. The winner is the first player to reach 'Finish'.

Extend the activity for older children by asking them to move back two or three places if they land on a holly leaf.

PAGE 86
CHRISTMAS EVE COUNTING

Learning objective
To inspire collating, recording and number recognition. (Mathematical Development)
Group size
Individuals or small groups.

Give each child a copy of the photocopiable sheet. Encourage them to count how many stockings, presents, crackers and candles there are in the picture, and to use the number line to help them write the correct answers in the appropriate boxes. Encourage the children to identify and record the number on the number line that they have not used. When they have filled in all the boxes, invite them to colour the scene.

PAGE 87
CHRISTMAS DECORATIONS

Learning objective
To reinforce shape-matching skills. (Mathematical Development)
Group size
Individuals or small groups.

Provide each child with a copy of the photocopiable sheet and invite them to choose four different colours to complete the colour code. Help them to follow their code to colour in the shapes on the tree. Encourage the children to name the shapes.

PAGE 88
WINTER SUN

Learning objective
To sequence a set of events. (Knowledge and Understanding of the World)
Group size
Individuals or small groups.

Provide each child with a copy of the photocopiable sheet and help them to cut it into four separate pictures. Invite the children to stick the pictures along a strip of card in the correct order to show the snowman gradually melting.

Encourage the children to talk about why the snowman is melting.

PAGE 89
MELTING!

Learning objective
To observe and record ice melting. (Knowledge and Understanding of the World)
Group size
Small groups.

Give each child a copy of the photocopiable sheet. Provide the group with an ice-cube or an ice-lolly in a bowl. Invite the children to draw what they see. Leave the ice in a warm place. Invite the children to keep an eye on the ice over a period of time. (As there is no time limit to the melting process, engage the children in other flexible activities nearby which they can break away from to make their observations.)

When the ice has completely melted, encourage the children to draw their second picture on their sheet.

Use the activity to inspire an awareness of how water in lakes and ponds can freeze and melt according to the temperature. Reinforce the dangers involved if people tread on frozen lakes and ponds.

PAGE 90
NEW YEAR'S CARD

Learning objective
To gain awareness of a yearly event and celebration. (Knowledge and Understanding of the World)
Group size
Individuals or small groups.

Talk with the children about events which occur once a year such as birthdays, Easter, Christmas and other religious festivals which are particularly relevant to your group.

Explain that people also celebrate each New Year and send cards to each other to wish them good luck and good health for the coming year.

An adult should prepare in advance for this activity by trimming off a section measuring approximately 3cm from the rims of several, used, clean, yoghurt pots, to create horseshoe shapes. Explain to the children that this shape represents good luck.

Provide each child with a copy of the photocopiable sheet and different-coloured paints in trays. Invite the children to print a colourful array of good luck horseshoe shapes on their sheet using the trimmed yoghurt pots.

Help the children to stick their design onto folded card, and to write a message inside.

PAGE 91
WINTER WEATHER GAME

Learning objective
To encourage gross motor skills and the ability to play fairly. (Physical Development)
Group size
Large groups.

Make two copies of the photocopiable sheet, enlarged to A3 size. Cut both sheets to create two sets of four pictures. Mount the pictures onto folded card.

Take the children to a room where they can move around freely and safely. Place four PE mats on the floor, spaced well apart. Fold the first set of cards so that the pictures are on the front, and stand them on a table. Place an instrument next to each picture and explain that each weather condition has its own sound.
For example:
• a triangle for snowflakes
• a drum for thunder and lightning
• a shaker for rain
• wooden blocks for hailstones.

Fold the second set of cards so that the pictures are hidden on the inside. Tuck one card under each mat.

Invite the children to move around the room in a specified way, such as hopping, in the same direction.

After a short while, make a noise using one of the four instruments, such as a few loud bangs on the drum to represent thunder. The children should immediately choose one mat to sit on, as a place to 'hide' from the thunder. When all the children are seated, let them remove the picture cards from under the mats to reveal where the thunder is. All the children who are 'hiding' on the thunder mat have been caught in the thunderstorm. These children should sit out for the next round. Replace the cards and repeat.

To maintain the element of surprise for the children, shuffle the cards before replacing them. To encourage memory skills, replace the cards under the same mat each time.

Learning objective
To help develop manual dexterity. (Physical Development)
Group size
Small or large groups.

PAGE 92
PAPER CHAINS

Give each child a copy of the photocopiable sheet. Encourage them to colour in the patterns using felt-tipped pens or pencils. Invite them to add coloured glitter, small shapes cut from shiny paper or sequins.

Help the children to cut along the lines to produce three separate strips. Show the children how to loop and glue the strips together to form a paper chain with three links. Invite several children to link their small chains together to produce one long chain. Use the paper chain to decorate the room during the run up to Christmas or for seasonal parties.

Learning objective
To inspire pencil control and pre-writing skills. (Physical Development)
Group size
Individuals or small groups.

PAGE 93
PATTERNED SCARVES

Give each child a copy of the photocopiable sheet and sharp coloured pencils. Encourage them to use the pencils to follow the letter patterns in the direction of the arrows. Ask them to copy the patterns to decorate the second, empty scarf.

Help the children to cut their photocopiable sheet in half to provide two scarves. Display several scarves, end to end, around the edges of a display board to create an unusual frame or border for the children's artwork on the theme of winter.

Learning objective
To inspire an imaginative use of colour and pattern. (Creative Development)
Group size
Individuals or small groups.

PAGE 94
WINTER BOOTS

Enlarge the photocopiable sheet to A3 size. Provide each child with a sheet, a selection of different-coloured paints and a variety of different-shaped printing materials.

Invite the children to print colourful shapes and patterns on the winter boots. Encourage older children to make symmetrical patterns or repeated patterns. Let younger children print random patterns.

Display several pairs of decorated boots in the area that you use for storing the children's boots in winter. Alternatively, mount them along the wall at floor level to create an unusual and colourful frieze.

Learning objective
To inspire creative imagination. (Creative Development)
Group size
Small groups.

PAGE 95
A WINTER FLOWER

Look at pictures of winter flowers, or if possible, real winter flowers.

Provide each child with an A4 or enlarged copy of the photocopiable sheet. Invite them to design and decorate an original winter flower using a range of coloured pens, pencils or collage materials such as sticky paper, tissue, fabric, wrapping paper, lace, shiny paper and crêpe paper. Alternatively, provide paints and a range of printing materials.

Create an interesting winter display by sticking several flowers along a strip of crumpled white fabric to represent a bed of snow.

Add a dark blue background speckled with painted snowflakes to enhance the wintry atmosphere.

Learning objective
To encourage colouring, cutting, gluing and decorating skills. (Creative Development)
Group size
Individual or small groups.

PAGE 96
SNOWSCENE MOBILE

If possible, show the children some examples of snowscene toys. (These are usually water-filled plastic domes containing a 3-D winter scene. A snowfall effect is produced when they are shaken.)

Give each child a copy of the photocopiable sheet. Invite them to draw and colour in the front and back view of a winter scene using pens, pencils, crayons, oil pastels or paints. Encourage them to add white or silver glitter to the picture to represent a snowfall.

Help the children to cut out their picture, then fold the sheet in half and glue the two scenes back to back. Help them to punch a hole in the top of their picture and then to add a length of thread to create a snowscene mobile.

Valentine heart

◆ Decorate the heart using pens, paints and collage.

To _____

From _____

Winter birds

◆ Write or draw where you saw each bird.
Colour in the pictures.

robin	
sparrow	
blackbird	

Keeping warm

✂ ◆ Cut out the four pictures. Put them in order.

A winter's day

◆ Write what you can see, hear and feel on a winter's day.

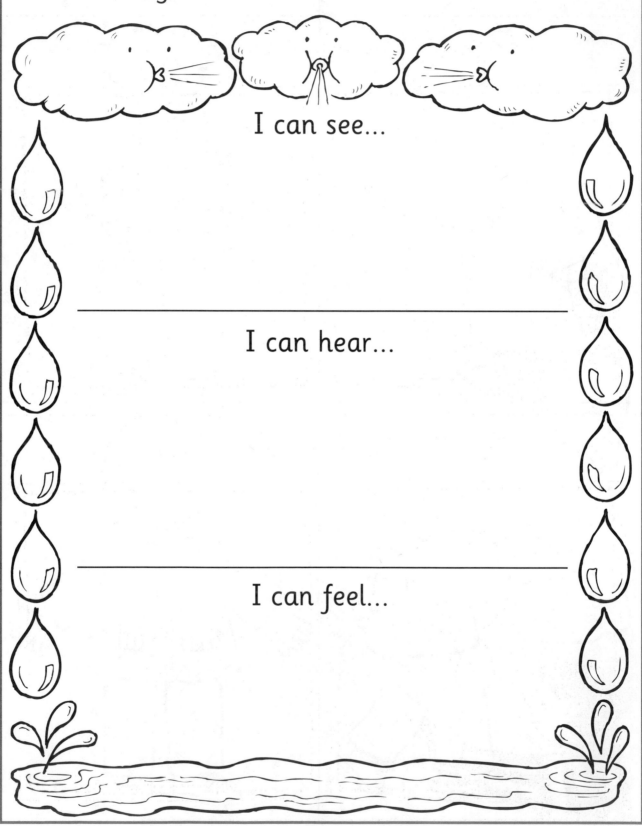

I can see...

I can hear...

I can feel...

Christmas Eve counting

◆ Use the number line to help you write the answers.

| 1 | 2 | 3 | 4 | 5 | 6 |

How many?

Which number is left over?

Snowman story

◆ Draw the snowman at night and the melted snowman in the morning.

Glue curtains here

Glue curtains here

Chilly words

◆ Write some winter words in the spaces on the snowflake.

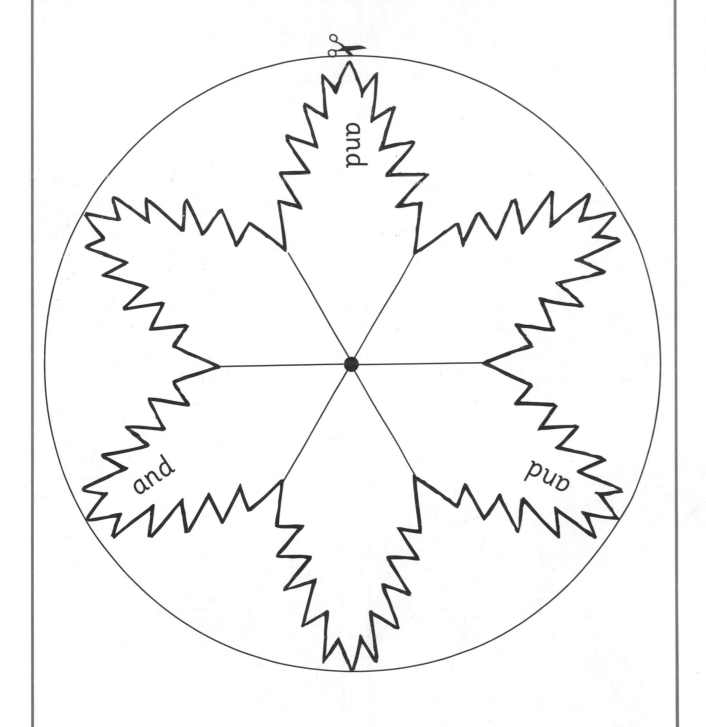

Holly and ivy game

◆ Write the numbers 1 to 10 and colour the berries red and the leaves green.

Start

Finish

Christmas decorations

◆ Make up your own colour code. Follow your code to decorate the tree.

Colour code

Winter sun

◆ Cut out the four pictures and stick them in the correct order.

Melting!

◆ Draw what you can see.

Name _____

My _____ looks like this.

Now it has melted, it looks like this.

New Year's card

◆ Design your own card for New Year.

Winter weather game

◆ Cut into four pictures.

snowflakes

thunder and lightning

raindrops

hailstones

Paper chains

◆ Colour in and cut out the three strips.

Glue here

Glue here

Glue here

92
WINTER

Patterned scarves

◆ Draw over the dotted lines. Copy the patterns to decorate the empty scarf.

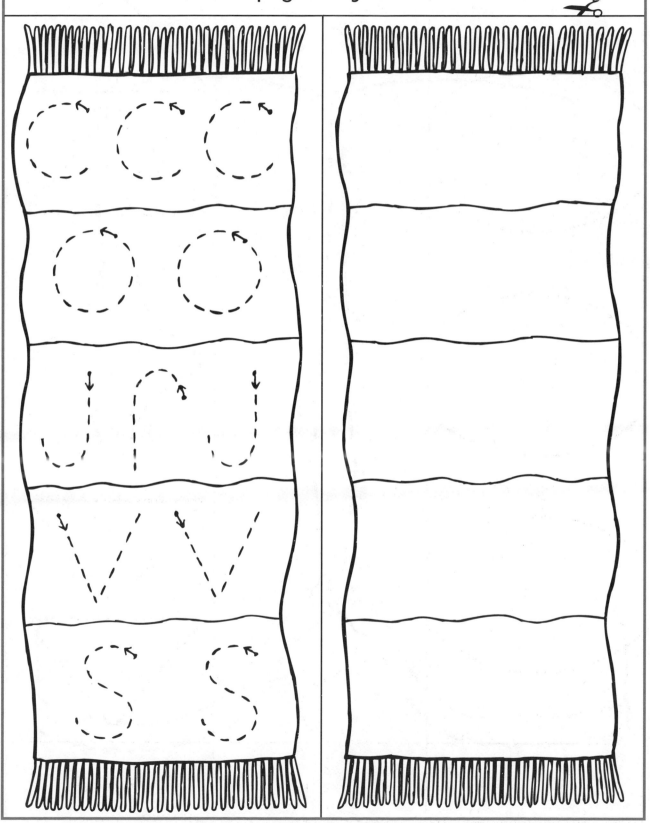

Winter boots

◆ Create your own design on these winter boots.

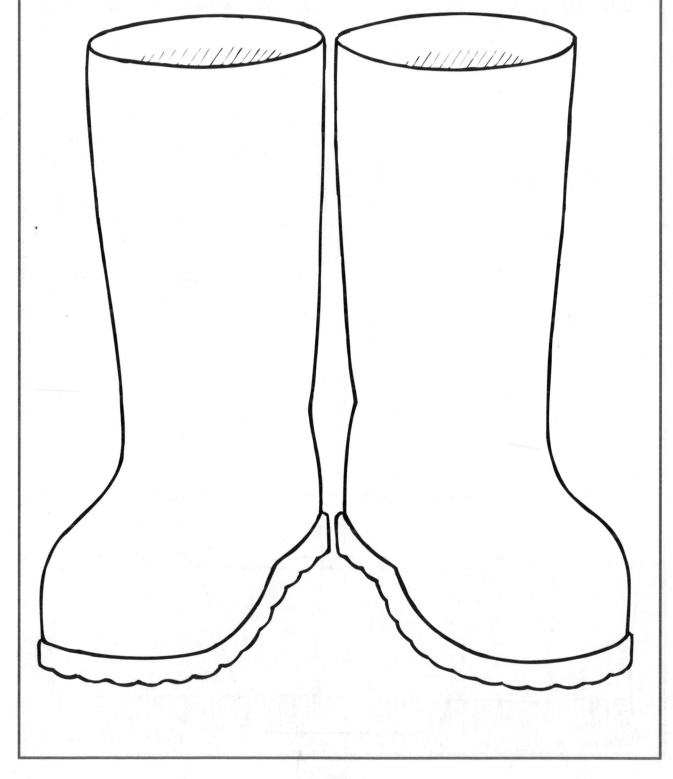

A winter flower

◆ Design and decorate an imaginary winter flower.

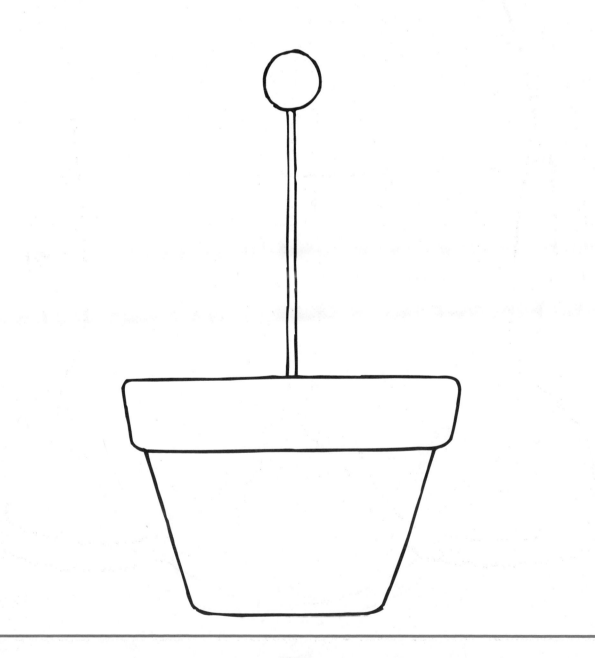

Snowscene mobile

◆ Draw the front and back of your scene. Sprinkle with glitter.

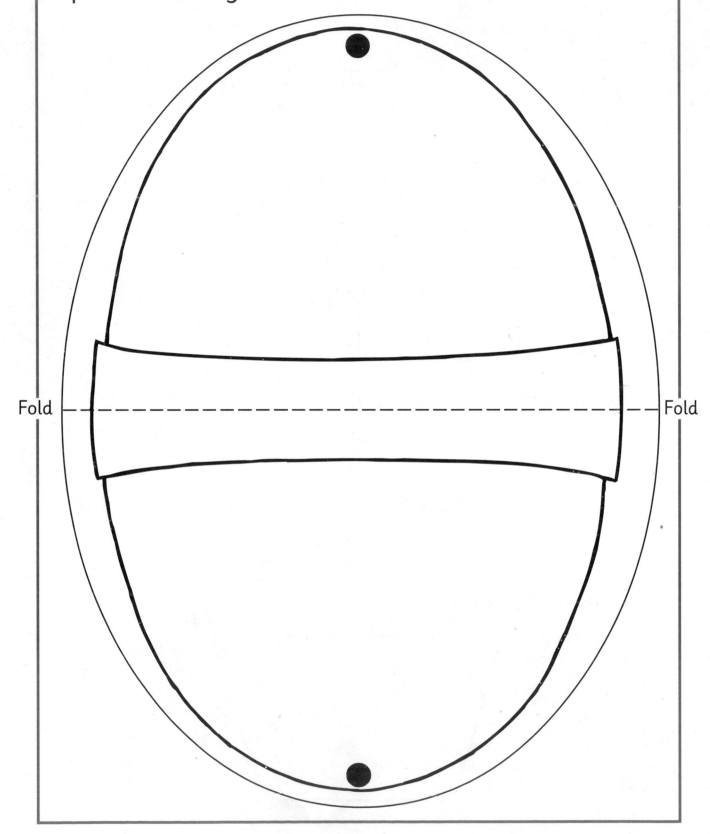

Fold – Fold